Best Linux distributions for desktop

Linux is an Operating system that is being used widely on Computers and servers worldwide. Not only it's free, but also an open-source project. Which means the source code of the Linux project is publicly available. Anyone can download these Linux distributions (distros) and modify them as they see fit.

Hence there are many popular Linux distributions out there, Such as Ubuntu, Linux Mint, and Fedora. When it comes to choosing the best distro for you, it's better to have an overall idea about below factors

- **User interface**: Although some Linux versions have user interfaces that are similar to those of other well-known operating systems (like Windows or macOS), others stand out more. If you're new to Linux, it could be easier to transfer if you pick a distribution with a recognizable interface.

- **Software availability**: Different Linux distributions have varying pre-installed applications, and some are better suited for particular tasks than others (such as gaming or programming). Choose a distribution that either already includes the software you require or makes it simple to install new software..
- **Hardware compatibility**: It's crucial to select a Linux distribution that is compatible with your hardware because some Linux distributions are made to run well on particular types of hardware (such as older computers or newer laptops with particular capabilities).

With these factors in mind, here are a few popular Linux distros that are well-suited for desktop use:

- **Ubuntu**: is one of the most popular Linux distros, and also there is much pre-installed common software, and it's supported by a wide range of hardware.
- **Linux Mint**: Another great distribution, Linux Mint is a very reliable distro, and comes with a Windows-like user interface, which increases user-friendliness as most of the common users are familiar with the user interface of Windows OS.
- **Fedora**: known for its focus on innovation and cutting-edge features, is mostly used by developers. This version includes the next-generation features before those are getting released for other distributions. The updates for this distro are comparatively more frequent than other distros. And we can experience the cutting-edge features of this distribution.

Best Linux Distros for Servers and Enterprise,

Unlike other Operating systems, Linux Operating systems are known for their flexibility and reliability, stability, and most importantly security. Hence various Linux distributions are being used in the Production environment for wide a range of purposes. Including Servers, Desktops, and also in embedded systems.

Below are the few factors why organizations trust Linux Operating Systems to run their operations.

- **Customization:** Utilizing a Linux distribution in a production setting has many benefits, one of them being the flexibility to modify the operating system to suit the unique demands of the organization. This might involve setting up particular programs and equipment, adjusting the operating system's settings to adhere to particular security and performance standards, and writing original scripts to automate procedures.

- **Security:** Linux distributions are known for their strong security features, which make them a popular choice for product surroundings. numerous distributions receive regular updates to address potential vulnerabilities and improve security. In addition, Linux distributions offer a number of security features such as firewalls, encryption tools, and access controls to help cover against cyber threats.

- **Stability:** Because downtime may have major repercussions in commercial contexts, Linux distributions are renowned for their reliability, which is essential. Numerous distributions are built with performance and reliability in mind and are intended for use in mission-critical situations.

- **Performance:** Linux distributions are also renowned for their speed, which makes them a suitable option for using tools and apps that need a lot of resources. Moreover, Linux distributions provide a variety of utilities and tools for improving system performance, such as tools for monitoring resource utilization and identifying bottlenecks.

- **Support:** In the event that there are any troubles or concerns with the server, it is important to have access to reliable support. Take into account the distribution's degree of support, including the existence of a dedicated support staff or community and the availability of paid assistance solutions.

- **Compatibility:** Verify the distribution's compatibility with the hardware and applications you intend to use for the server. This relates to compatibility with the CPU architecture as well.

Once we considered the requirements in detail, we have a few well-known distributions to proceed with.

- **Red Hat Enterprise Linux (RHEL)**

RHEL is ideal for mission-critical environments where downtime might have serious repercussions. RHEL offers a variety of support options, including the option to pay RedHat for specialized support staff to solve any server-related problems.

Additionally, RHEL aids in meeting particular compliance standards. RHEL is frequently used in regulated businesses like banking and healthcare, where compliance standards are essential.

RHEL is a solid option all around for businesses looking for a supported, reliable, and stable operating system for their production servers. It is best suited for regulated sectors, mission-critical environments, and configurations that require a certain set of tools or apps.

- **CentOS**

CentOS is a community-supported Linux distribution that's based on Red Hat Enterprise Linux (RHEL). It's a stable and reliable distribution that's often used in servers and enterprise environments. Here are some situations when you might consider using CentOS

1. When you need a stable and reliable operating system Like RHEL - CentOS is known for its stability and reliability, making it a good choice for mission-critical surroundings where downtime can have serious consequences.

2. When you want a free alternative to RHEL - CentOS is available as open-source software and can be freely downloaded and used. This can be a good choice for organizations that are looking to reduce operating costs but still want a stable and reliable operating system.

3. When you need to run specific operations or tools - CentOS is based on RHEL, which means it's compatible with a wide range of operations and tools. This makes it a good choice for environments where specific operations or tools are needed.

4. When you want a distribution with a strong community - CentOS has a strong community of users and developers who contribute to the design and give support. This can be a good resource for getting help and advice when using CentOS.

- **Ubuntu**

    Ubuntu is a stable and reliable Linux distribution that's extensively used in both desktop and server environments. It's known for its user-friendly interface and ease of use, and it receives regular updates to address potential vulnerabilities and improve stability. In addition, Ubuntu has a large and active community of users and inventors who contribute to the design and provide support.

    Another reason to choose ubuntu is, the most popular centos 8 reached its end of life (EOL) on May 31, 2021, which means that it's no longer receiving updates or support from the CentOS project. This has led many associations to consider alternative distributions, and Ubuntu is a popular choice for numerous of them.

still, it can be a good alternative to CentOS for a product server, If the applications and tools that your association uses are compatible with Ubuntu. still, it's important to carefully estimate whether Ubuntu meets the specific requirements and conditions of your association before making a decision.

- **Debian**

Debian and Ubuntu are quite similar; in fact, Ubuntu is based on Debian. The majority of the features included in Debian are also found in Ubuntu.

However, there are also instances when certain apps can only be operated on Debian. In these cases, it is preferable to only utilize Debian as the server operating system.

Best Linux Distributions for Hacking and Penetration Testing

There are a number of Linux distributions that are specifically designed for use in hacking and penetration testing. Some of the most popular options include

- **Kali Linux**: Kali Linux is an extensively used distribution that is specifically designed for ethical hacking and penetration testing. It comes with a wide range of tools for tasks similar to network scanning, password cracking, and vulnerability assessment.

- **BlackArch**: BlackArch is a distribution created based on top of Arch Linux, and it comes with a large collection of tools for penetration testing and ethical hacking. It has over 2000 tools available for tasks such as network scanning and password cracking.

- **Parrot OS**: Parrot OS is a Debian-based security-focused distribution that is designed for use in ethical hacking, penetration testing, and other security-related tasks. It includes a wide range of tools and features that make it well-suited for these purposes.

- **BackBox**: BackBox is a well-known Linux distribution that is based on Ubuntu and is designed for use in penetration testing and ethical hacking. This OS has a variety of capabilities and tools for pen testing, just like the other Operating Systemsdes described in this section.

It's important to note that while these distributions can be useful for learning about and testing the security of computer systems, it's illegal to use them to gain unauthorized access to systems or to perform malicious activities. It's important to use these tools ethically and in agreement with the law.

Shortcut for terminal

The terminal can be used with a variety of keyboard shortcuts to make it simpler to use and navigate. Here are a few typical examples:

Ctrl + A: Move the cursor to the beginning of the line

Ctrl + E: Move the cursor to the end of the line

Ctrl + U: Clear the line before the cursor

Ctrl + K: Clear the line after the cursor

Ctrl + W: Delete the word before the cursor

Ctrl + L: Clear the terminal screen

Ctrl + C: Terminate the current command

Ctrl + D: Exit the terminal

Remember that these shortcuts may vary based on your operating system and terminal. Ctrl + Shift +? or a glance at the terminal's settings or documentation will typically yield a list of the possible shortcuts.

Text editors are one of the key tools we commonly encounter on Linux-based operating systems. Therefore, it is better to be aware of the standard text editor shortcuts.

Here are a few VIM editing shortcuts.

I	: Enter insert mode, which allows you to edit the text
Esc	: Exit insert mode and return to command mode
x	: Delete the character under the cursor
dd	: Delete the current line
u	: Undo the last change
Ctrl + R	: Redo the last change
/	: Search for a specific word or phrase in the document
:w	: Save the current document
:q	: Exit Vim

You can change the key bindings to suit your needs and choose from a wide variety of additional shortcuts for Vim. By typing :help or reviewing the Vim manual, you can also get a list of the shortcuts that are available.

Install dual-boot with both Windows and Ubuntu

1. Although setting up a dual-boot system with Windows and Ubuntu is quite simple, it's crucial to follow the instructions precisely to prevent any problems. Here is a step-by-step tutorial for setting up a dual-boot system that runs Ubuntu and Windows:

2. Download the latest version of Ubuntu from the official website (https://ubuntu.com/download/desktop). Make sure to select the appropriate version for your computer's architecture (either 32-bit or 64-bit).

3. From the Ubuntu image, you obtained, create a bootable USB stick or DVD. To make a bootable USB device, use a program like Etcher (for Windows, Mac, or Linux) or Rufus (for Windows).

4. Back up all of your important data and files. Before making any system modifications, it's usually a good idea to keep a backup of your important data.

5. Start up your computer from the DVD or USB disk. To boot from the USB drive or DVD, you might need to change your boot order in the BIOS or UEFI settings.

6. Select "Install Ubuntu" when the Ubuntu installation screen displays, then follow the on-screen instructions to install Ubuntu on your computer. When asked how you want to install Ubuntu, make sure to choose "Install Ubuntu alongside Windows."

7. To finish the installation process, adhere to the instructions. This will involve setting up your time zone and keyboard layout in addition to creating a user account.

8. When the installation is finished, restart your computer and choose the desired operating system from the boot menu. You might need to adjust your boot order in the BIOS or UEFI settings if the boot menu doesn't show.

9. That's it! Now that Windows and Ubuntu are both installed, your computer should be dual-booting.

10. It's important to keep in mind that partitioning your hard drive will be required to install a dual-boot system, so you will need to have enough free space on your drive to fit both operating systems. Before installing Ubuntu, you might need to delete some files or make more room on your hard drive if you don't have enough free space.

Changing the Time Zone in Linux

One of the first things you might want to do when setting up a new OS is to change the time zone to match your location. This makes sure that the system clock is displaying the correct local time, which is vital for various tasks such as scheduling events and keeping track of log files.

In this chapter, you will learn the process of changing the time zone in Linux step by step.

Step 1: Determine the current time zone

Before we begin, it's important to know the current time zone of your system. You can check the current time zone by running the date command

```
$ date
Fri Mar 12 15:07:45 EST 2021
```

The output of the date command shows the current date and time, as well as the time zone (in this case, EST for Eastern Standard Time).

Step 2: Find your time zone in the tzdata database

Linux systems use a database of time zones called tzdata to determine the correct time for a given location. The tzdata database includes information on time zones all around the world, including their names and the offsets from Coordinated Universal Time (UTC).

To find the time zone that corresponds to your location, you can use the tzselect command. This command will ask you a series of questions about your location and then suggest a time zone that matches your answers:

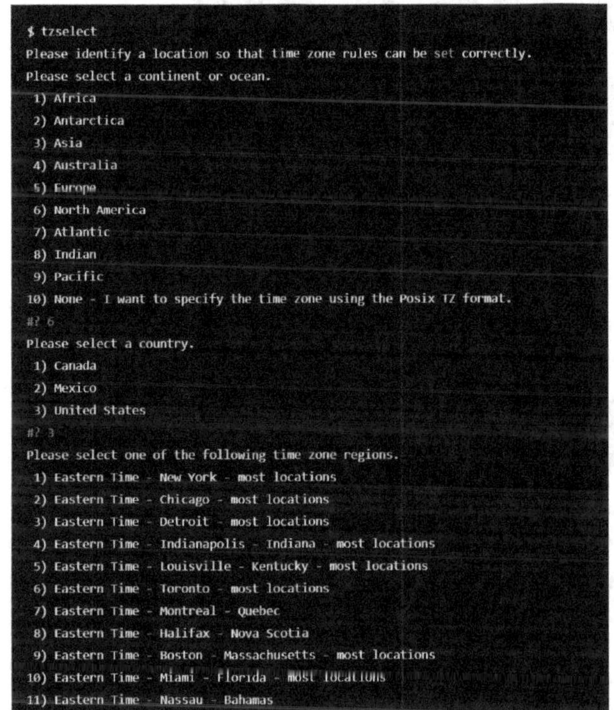

```
$ tzselect
Please identify a location so that time zone rules can be set correctly.
Please select a continent or ocean.
 1) Africa
 2) Antarctica
 3) Asia
 4) Australia
 5) Europe
 6) North America
 7) Atlantic
 8) Indian
 9) Pacific
10) None - I want to specify the time zone using the Posix TZ format.
#? 6
Please select a country.
 1) Canada
 2) Mexico
 3) United States
#? 3
Please select one of the following time zone regions.
 1) Eastern Time - New York - most locations
 2) Eastern Time - Chicago - most locations
 3) Eastern Time - Detroit - most locations
 4) Eastern Time - Indianapolis - Indiana - most locations
 5) Eastern Time - Louisville - Kentucky - most locations
 6) Eastern Time - Toronto - most locations
 7) Eastern Time - Montreal - Quebec
 8) Eastern Time - Halifax - Nova Scotia
 9) Eastern Time - Boston - Massachusetts - most locations
10) Eastern Time - Miami - Florida - most locations
11) Eastern Time - Nassau - Bahamas
```

```
11) Eastern Time - Nassau - Bahamas
12) Eastern Time - Kingston - Jamaica
13) Eastern Time - Havana - Cuba
14) Eastern Time - Florida Keys - Florida
15) Eastern Time - Port-au-Prince - Haiti
16) Eastern Time - Kingston - Saint Vincent and the Grenadines
17) Eastern Time - Caracas - Venezuela
#? 1

The following information has been given:
    Eastern Time - New York - most locations

Therefore TZ='America/New_York' will be used.
Local time is now:      Fri Mar 12 15:07:45 EST 2021.
Universal Time is now:  Fri Mar 12 20:07:45 UTC 2021.
Is the above information OK?
#? y
```

The **tzselect** command will output a string in the format TZ='<timezone>', which represents the time zone that matches your location.

Step 3: Set the time zone using the TZ environment variable

Once you have determined the correct time zone for your location, you can use the TZ environment variable to set the time zone for your system. To set the time zone, you can use the export command to set the TZ variable in your shell

```
$ export TZ='America/New_York'
```

Note that the TZ variable must be set in quotes to avoid any issues with spaces or special characters in the time zone name.

Step 4: Verify the time zone change

To verify that the time zone has been changed, you can run the date command again:

```
$ date
Fri Mar 12 15:07:45 EST 2021
```

You should see the time zone in the output of the date command has changed to the new time zone you set.

Step 5: Make the time zone change permanent

The time zone change you just made using the TZ environment variable is only temporary and will be lost when you log out or reboot your system. To make the time zone change permanent, you need to update the system-wide time zone configuration file.

On most Linux systems, the system-wide time zone configuration file is located at /etc/localtime. To update this file, you can use the ln command to create a symbolic link from /etc/localtime to the correct time zone file in the tzdata database:

```
$ sudo ln -sf /usr/share/zoneinfo/America/New_York /etc/localtime
```

This command creates a symbolic link from /etc/localtime to the /usr/share/zoneinfo/America/New_York file, which is the time zone file for the Eastern Time zone in the United States.

Step 6: Verify the permanent time zone change

To verify that the time zone change has been made permanent, you can run the date command again

```
$ date
Fri Mar 12 15:07:45 EST 2021
```

You should see the time zone in the output of the date command is still set to the new time zone you set.

Congratulations! You have successfully changed the time zone on your Linux system.

Working with Filesystem Commands

1. Navigating the filesystem:

    - To navigate to a different directory, use the **cd** (change directory) command followed by the path to the desired directory.
    - To see the contents of the current directory, use the **ls** (list) command.
    - To see the directory structure starting from the current directory, use the tree command.
    - To go back to the parent directory, use **cd ..**
    - To go to the home directory, use **cd ~**

2. Creating and deleting files and directories:

    - To create a new file, use the **touch** command followed by the desired file name.
    - To create a new directory, use the **mkdir** (make directory) command followed by the desired directory name.
    - To delete a file, use the **rm** (remove) command followed by the file name.
    - To delete an empty directory, use the **rmdir** (remove directory) command followed by the directory name.
    - To delete a directory and all its contents, use the **rm -r** command followed by the directory name.

3. Copying and moving files and directories:

    - To copy a file, use the **cp** (copy) command followed by the source file and destination file/directory.
    - To copy a directory and its contents, use the **cp -r** command followed by the source directory and destination directory.
    - To move a file, use the **mv** (move) command followed by the source file and destination file/directory.
    - To move a directory and its contents, use the **mv** command followed by the source directory and destination directory.

4. Viewing and editing files:

- To view the contents of a file, use the **cat** (concatenate) command followed by the file name.
- To view the contents of a file one page at a time, use the **less** command followed by the file name.
- To edit a file, use a text editor such as **nano** or **vi**.

A few more commonly used commands

1. **pwd** (print working directory): This command displays the full path of the current directory.

2. **ln** (link): This command creates a link to a file or directory. There are two types of links: hard links and soft links. A hard link creates a new name for an existing file, while a soft link creates a pointer to the file. To create a hard link, use ln source_file destination_link, and to create a soft link, use **ln -s source_file destination_link**.

3. **find**: This command searches for files and directories based on specified criteria. For example, **find / -name '*.txt'** will search for all text files starting from the root directory.

4. **grep** (global regular expression print): This command searches for a specific pattern in one or more files. For example, **grep 'error' logfile.txt** will search for the pattern 'error' in the file 'logfile.txt'.

5. **tar** (tape archive): This command is used to create and extract archives. To create an archive, use **tar -cf archive.tar file1 file2**, and to extract an archive, use tar -xf archive.tar.

Working with Permission

Every file and directory in Linux operating system includes a set of permissions associated with it that manages who is allowed to access it. These permissions ar given as a mix of 3 types: read, write, and execute.

The **read** permission permits a user to view the contents of the file. this suggests that if a user has read permission for a file, they can use commands like "cat" or "less" to look at the file's contents.

The **write** permission permits a user to form changes to the file. this suggests that if a user has the write permission for a file, they can use commands like "nano" or "vi" to edit the file.

The **execute** permission permits a user to execute the file as a program. this suggests that if a user has the execute permission for a file, they can run the file by typewriting its name into the program line.

In Linux, there are 3 levels of permissions: **owner**, **group**, and **others**. The owner is that the user who owns the file, the group may be a set of users who are a part of the same group as the owner, and others refer to all other users on the system.

You can read the permissions of a file or directory using the "ls -al" command. this may show a listing of files and directories (including hidden files and directories), along with their permissions. The permissions are displayed within the variety of a 10-character string, with the primary character representing the sort of file (for example, "d" for a directory or "-" for a regular file) and therefore the remaining 9 characters representing the permissions for the owner, group, and others.

Below is an output from the "ls -al" command.

```
total 12
drwxr-xr-x  3 user  staff  102 Jan  1 16:00 .
drwxr-xr-x  7 user  staff  238 Jan  1 15:47 ..
-rw-r--r--  1 user  staff   18 Jan  1 16:00 file1.txt
-rw-r--r--  1 user  staff   23 Jan  1 16:00 file2.txt
drwxr-xr-x  2 user  staff   68 Jan  1 16:00 folder1
```

In this example, the "total 12" line indicates that there are 12 blocks of disk space used by the files and directories in the current directory. Each line represents a file or directory, with the following information:

- In Column 1, the first character indicates the type of file: "-" for a regular file, "d" for a directory, "l" for a symbolic link, etc.
- The next nine characters represent the permissions for the file or directory. In this example, the permissions are "rwxr-xr-x", which means that the owner has read, write, and execute permissions (rwx), the group has read and execute permissions (r-x), and others have read and execute permissions (r-x).
- Column 2 shows the number of links to the file.
- Column 3 shows the owner of the file.
- Column 4 shows the group that the owner belongs to.
- The next field shows the size of the file in bytes.
- The next field shows the date and time that the file was last modified.
- The final field shows the name of the file or directory.

To change the permissions of a file or directory, you'll use the "chmod" command. The "chmod" command permits you to specify the permissions you would like to set using either symbolic notation or octal notation.

In symbolic notation, you'll use the "+" or "-" characters to featuro or take away permissions, and therefore the "u", "g", and "o" characters to specify the owner, group, or others, severally. for instance, "chmod u+rw file.txt" would give the owner read and write permissions for the file "file.txt".

In octal notation, you'll specify the permissions as a three-digit number, with every digit representing the permissions for the owner, group, and others, severally. The digits are calculated by adding up the values for the permissions you would like to set. for instance, "chmod 744 file.txt" would offer the owner read, write, and execute permissions (7 = four + a pair of + 1), and provides everybody else read permissions (4 = 4).

In Linux, there's also the concept of the "setuid" and "setgid" bits, which permit a program to be executed with the permissions of the owner or group, respectively. These bits is set using the "chmod" command, using the "u" and "g" characters to specify the "setuid" and "setgid" bits, respectively.

Working with Linux Networking Commands

Linux offers a range of networking capabilities and tools that enable users to attach to networks and to the internet, share resources, and communicate with different devices.

In Linux, networking is managed through a set of configuration files and therefore the command interface (CLI). the primary configuration file for networking is /etc/network/interfaces (The path may vary depending on the OS you choose), which contains info regarding the network interfaces on a device and the way they should be configured. Such as the device IP address, Subnet mask, Gateway and etc.

Linux additionally includes many tools for managing and troubleshooting networks. These include ping, traceroute, netstat commands. Most of these packages are comes out of the box, and some of the commands have to be installed manually after the initial OS installation.

Linux additionally supports a large range of protocols, together with TCP/IP, the standard protocol for the internet, furthermore as various virtual private network (VPN) protocols. These protocols enable devices to communicate over the net and securely connect with remote networks.

Overall, Linux provides a sturdy and versatile platform for networking, creating it a preferred alternative for organizations and people alike.

Below are a few of the commonly used network-related commands used in the Linux Environment.

- **ifconfig** - Allows you to configure network interfaces. You can use it to view the status of your current network connections, assign an IP address to a network interface, and more.

```
eth0: flags=4163<UP,BROADCAST,RUNNING,MULTICAST>  mtu 1500
        inet 192.168.1.100  netmask 255.255.255.0  broadcast 192.168.1.255
        inet6 fe80::215:5dff:fe00.c00  prefixlen 64  scopeid 0x20<link>
        ether 00:15:5d:00:c0:00  txqueuelen 1000  (Ethernet)
        RX packets 36468  bytes 27303938 (26.0 MiB)
        RX errors 0  dropped 0  overruns 0  frame 0
        TX packets 24389  bytes 3329053 (3.1 MiB)
        TX errors 0  dropped 0 overruns 0  carrier 0  collisions 0

lo: flags=73<UP,LOOPBACK,RUNNING>  mtu 65536
        inet 127.0.0.1  netmask 255.0.0.0
        inet6 ::1  prefixlen 128  scopeid 0x10<host>
        loop  txqueuelen 1000  (Local Loopback)
        RX packets 1124  bytes 86560 (84.5 KiB)
        RX errors 0  dropped 0  overruns 0  frame 0
        TX packets 1124  bytes 86560 (84.5 KiB)
        TX errors 0  dropped 0 overruns 0  carrier 0  collisions 0
```

This output shows the status of two network interfaces on the system: eth0 (Ethernet) and lo (loopback). The ifconfig command displays information such as the IP addresses assigned to each interface, the MAC addresses, and the number of packets sent and received.

- **ping** - Allows you to test the connectivity between two devices. It can be either on the same network or on another network. You can use it to determine if another device is reachable and how long it takes for packets to travel between the two devices.

```
$ ping example.com
PING example.com (93.184.216.34) 56(84) bytes of data.
64 bytes from 93.184.216.34: icmp_seq=1 ttl=56 time=17.8 ms
64 bytes from 93.184.216.34: icmp_seq=2 ttl=56 time=18.5 ms
64 bytes from 93.184.216.34: icmp_seq=3 ttl=56 time=17.8 ms
64 bytes from 93.184.216.34: icmp_seq=4 ttl=56 time=18.5 ms

--- example.com ping statistics ---
4 packets transmitted, 4 received, 0% packet loss, time 3005ms
rtt min/avg/max/mdev = 17.839/18.111/18.588/0.352 ms
```

- **traceroute** - Allows you to track the path that packets take from your device to a destination on the internet. It can be useful for troubleshooting network issues or determining the location of a device on the network.

```
$ traceroute example.com
traceroute to example.com (93.184.216.34), 30 hops max, 60 byte packets
 1  192.168.1.1 (192.168.1.1)  1.672 ms  1.645 ms  1.620 ms
 2  10.0.0.1 (10.0.0.1)  8.578 ms  8.697 ms  8.798 ms
 3  10.0.1.1 (10.0.1.1)  13.253 ms  13.330 ms  13.452 ms
 4  172.16.0.1 (172.16.0.1)  16.998 ms  17.066 ms  17.144 ms
 5  * * *
 6  173.194.217.190 (173.194.217.190)  17.976 ms  17.984 ms  17.993 ms
 7  209.85.242.78 (209.85.242.78)  18.041 ms 209.85.242.74 (209.85.242.74)
18.094 ms 209.85.242.78 (209.85.242.78)  18.073 ms
 8  216.239.56.15 (216.239.56.15)  18.124 ms 216.239.56.11 (216.239.56.11)
18.089 ms 216.239.56.15 (216.239.56.15)  18.105 ms
 9  216.239.58.142 (216.239.58.142)  18.659 ms 216.239.58.138 (216.239.58.138)
18.653 ms 216.239.58.142 (216.239.58.142)  18.637 ms
10  108.170.250.147 (108.170.250.147)  20.913 ms 108.170.250.149
(108.170.250.149)  21.018 ms 108.170.250.153 (108.170.250.153)  21.171 ms
11  93.184.216.34 (93.184.216.34)  23.062 ms  23.087 ms  23.123 ms
```

The output shows the list of hops between your device and the destination, along with the IP address and round-trip time for each hop. If a hop cannot be reached, it is represented by an asterisk (*). The final hop should be the destination itself.

Note that traceroute works by sending packets with increasing time-to-live (TTL) values, so that each hop along the path will send an error message when the TTL expires. This allows traceroute to determine the path that the packets take through the network.

- **nslookup** - Allows you to query DNS (Domain Name System) servers to find the IP address associated with a domain name or the domain name associated with an IP address.

```
$ nslookup example.com
Server:      192.168.1.1
Address:     192.168.1.1#53

Non-authoritative answer:
Name:    example.com
Address: 93.184.216.34
```

In this example, the nslookup command queried the DNS server at 192.168.1.1 and received a response indicating that the IP address for "example.com" is 93.184.216.34.

You can also use nslookup to perform reverse lookups, by specifying an IP address instead of a domain name

Ex : $nslookup 93.184.216.34
This would return the domain name associated with the IP address, if one is available.

- **netstat** - Allows you to view network statistics and the status of network connections. You can see which ports are open on your device and which connections are active.

  The routing table can also be printed using Netstat. We have a variety of options at our disposal to customize the result. Two of the most typical uses for netstat are shown below. (You can change the output of the netstat command by changing the required options)

  - Netstat command with -tnupl options (order of the options is irrelevant in this command)

    -n: Show numerical addresses instead of resolving them to hostnames.

    -t: Display TCP connections.

    -u: Display UDP connections.

    -p: Show the PID and name of the program associated with each connection.

    -l: Only show listening sockets.

```
$ netstat -ntupl
Active Internet connections (only servers)
Proto Recv-Q Send-Q Local Address           Foreign Address         State
PID/Program name
tcp        0      0 0.0.0.0:22              0.0.0.0:*               LISTEN
1067/sshd
tcp        0      0 0.0.0.0:80              0.0.0.0:*               LISTEN
1085/httpd
tcp        0      0 127.0.0.1:25            0.0.0.0:*               LISTEN
1046/sendmail
tcp6       0      0 :::22                   :::*                    LISTEN
1067/sshd
tcp6       0      0 :::80                   :::*                    LISTEN
1085/httpd
tcp6       0      0 ::1:25                  :::*                    LISTEN
1046/sendmail
udp        0      0 0.0.0.0:68              0.0.0.0:*
1071/dhclient
udp        0      0 0.0.0.0:123             0.0.0.0:*
1043/ntpd
udp6       0      0 :::123                  :::*
1043/ntpd
```

- **route** - Allows you to view and manipulate the routing table on your device. You can use it to view the routes that traffic takes to reach its destination and add or delete routes as needed. (Below is a sample output)

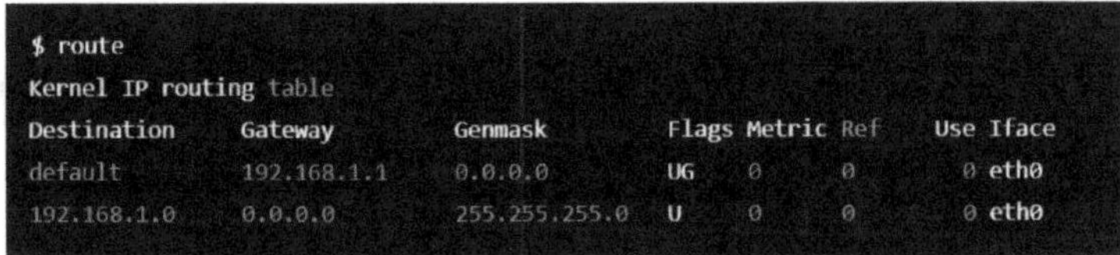

```
$ route
Kernel IP routing table
Destination     Gateway         Genmask          Flags Metric Ref    Use Iface
default         192.168.1.1     0.0.0.0          UG    0      0        0 eth0
192.168.1.0     0.0.0.0         255.255.255.0    U     0      0        0 eth0
```

This output shows the destination and gateway for each route, along with the interface through which the traffic will be sent. The "Genmask" column indicates the subnet mask for the destination. The "Flags" column shows the status of the route, with "U" indicating that the route is up.

You can also use the route command to add or delete routes from the routing table. For example, to add a new route to the table, you can use the add command like this:

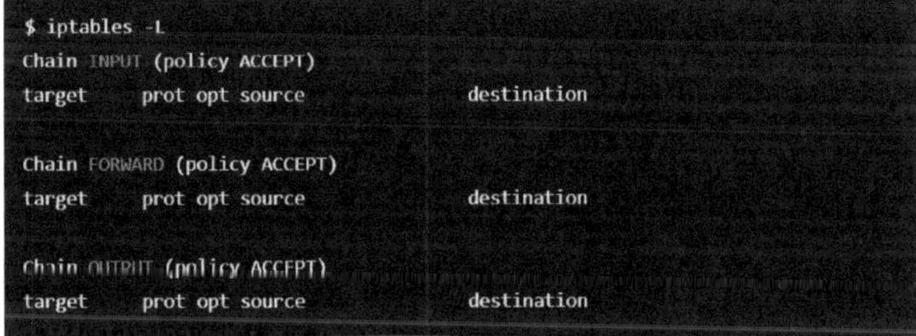

```
route add -net 10.0.0.0 netmask 255.0.0.0 gw 192.168.1.1 dev eth0
```

- **iptables** - Allows you to configure the firewall on your device. You can use it to set rules for incoming and outgoing traffic, block specific IP addresses or ports, and more.

```
$ iptables -L
Chain INPUT (policy ACCEPT)
target     prot opt source               destination

Chain FORWARD (policy ACCEPT)
target     prot opt source               destination

Chain OUTPUT (policy ACCEPT)
target     prot opt source               destination
```

This output shows the three default chains in the firewall: INPUT, FORWARD, and OUTPUT. Each chain has a default policy (ACCEPT in this case) that determines what to do with packets that don't match any of the rules in the chain.

To add a new rule to the firewall, you can use the iptables command with the -A option. For example, to block all incoming traffic from a specific IP address, you can use the following command:

```
iptables -A INPUT -s 1.2.3.4 -j DROP
```

This will add a rule to the INPUT chain that drops any packets coming from the IP address 1.2.3.4.

To delete a rule from the firewall, you can use the iptables command with the -D option. For example, to delete the rule we just added, you can use the following command:

```
iptables -D INPUT -s 1.2.3.4 -j DROP
```

This will remove the rule from the INPUT chain.

Working with Linux Update-Upgrade Commands

Before you begin, it is usually a good plan to make sure your system is up to date. To do this, you'll use the apt update command. This command retrieves new lists of packages and their dependencies from the package repositories and updates them on your system.

Once the package lists are updated, you can use the apt upgrade command to install any available updates. This command will install newer versions of packages that are already installed on your system, furthermore as any new dependencies that are needed.

You can also use the apt dist-upgrade command to upgrade your system to a newer version of the Linux distribution. This command will handle any dependencies and conflicts that may arise throughout the upgrade process.

If you wish to upgrade a specific package, you can use the apt install command followed by the package name. as an example, to upgrade the bash package, you'd use the command apt install bash.

To remove a package that's now not required, you can use the apt remove command followed by the package name. as an example, to remove the bash package, you'd use the command apt remove bash.

If you wish to completely take away a package and its configuration files, you can use the apt purge command followed by the package name. this can be useful if you wish to get rid of a package and every one of its associated configuration files.

Working with User Administration

There are several things to consider while dealing with User Administration, as well as some best practices to follow when managing users. The following are some things to think about when creating users.

Factors to consider before creating users

- Determine what the user accounts' purposes are. Will the users be external or internal partners or employees? This will enable you to choose the degree of access that is best for them.
- Identify the user characteristics that are required. Information including a person's name, email address, job title, and the department may be included.
- Create user accounts. Typically, this essentially gives each user a username and password and assigns the proper groups or responsibilities for them.
- Identify each user's access level. Will the user be able to access all resources and systems, or will access be limited in some way?
- Observe user behavior. It's crucial to often monitor user account activity to make sure they are being utilized properly and to spot any possible security risks.
- As required, update user accounts. This might entail changing user characteristics, resetting passwords, or denying access to individuals who have left the firm.

Best Practices

- Use secure passwords that are unique for every user. As a result, password cracking and unauthorized access will be mitigated
- Give high-level accounts two-factor authentication. Asking users to submit an additional form of authentication in addition to their password, offers an extra degree of protection.
- Review and update user access on a regular basis. Users who have left the firm should have their access levels revised, and existing users should have their access levels modified as needed.
- Observe user behavior. Continually monitor user account activity to make sure they are being utilized properly and to spot any possible security risks.

- Use separate accounts for various needs. For instance, create different accounts for general usage and administrative activities.
- It's easy to use groups to manage access to resources, instead of dealing with individual user permissions. This will make it easier to manage access for multiple users at once.

Below are a few of the commands that we can use to create and manage users.

- Create a new user

adduser: In Ubuntu, you can use the adduser command to create a new user. For example, to create a new user called newuser, you can use the following command.

```
sudo adduser newuser
```

This will prompt you to ontor a password for the user, as well as some other information such as the user's full name and contact details.

- Change password

passwd: This command allows you to change a user's password. For example, to change the password for the user newuser, you can use the following command.

```
sudo passwd newuser
```

- Modify Existing user

usermod: This command allows you to modify the attributes of a user account, such as the user's name, home directory, and primary group. For example, to change the primary group of the user newuser to admin, you can use the following command.

```
sudo usermod -g admin newuser
```

- Add a new group

addgroup: This command allows you to create a new group. For example, to create a new group called admin, you can use the following command.

```
sudo addgroup admin
```

- Delete a user

deluser: This command allows you to delete a user account. For example, to delete the user newuser, you can use the following command.

```
sudo deluser newuser
```

Working with Disk Usage

Management of disk space: By keeping an eye on your disk utilization, you can make sure that there is enough free space for your system to run efficiently. The biggest files and folders can be removed or moved to another drive if the disk is about to fill up.

Performance: As the system is working harder to discover available space to write new data, a full disk might result in lower performance. By monitoring disk utilization, you may locate and fix any performance issues before they worsen.

Troubleshooting: If you are experiencing issues with your system, checking disk usage can help you identify the root cause. For example, if a disk is full, it could be causing issues with the system's ability to write new data.

Capacity planning: By regularly checking disk usage, you can get a better understanding of your storage needs over time. This can help you plan for future upgrades or the addition of new disks.

Below are some basic commands that will be useful when checking disk spaces.

1. Viewing disk usage

You can use the df command to view the disk usage of your file systems. The -h flag displays the sizes in "human-readable" format, making it easier to read

For example:

```
$ df -h
Filesystem      Size  Used Avail Use% Mounted on
/dev/sda1       477G   12G  445G   3% /
devtmpfs        3.9G     0  3.9G   0% /dev
tmpfs           3.9G  8.0K  3.9G   1% /dev/shm
tmpfs           3.9G  4.0M  3.9G   1% /run
tmpfs           3.9G     0  3.9G   0% /sys/fs/cgroup
/dev/sdb1       917G  738G  179G  81% /mnt/disk2
```

The df command displays the file system, the total size, the used space, the available space, and the usage percentage.

2. Checking inode usage

In addition to disk space, you can also check the usage of inodes on your file systems. Inodes store information about files and directories on a file system. You can use the df -i command to view inode usage.

For example:

```
$ df -i
Filesystem        Inodes  IUsed    IFree IUse% Mounted on
/dev/sda1       12582912 719600 11864312    6% /
devtmpfs         9954560    492  9954368    1% /dev
tmpfs            9993216      1  9993215    1% /dev/shm
tmpfs            9993216    577  9987639    1% /run
tmpfs            9993216      3  9993213    1% /sys/fs/cgroup
/dev/sdb1       26214400 844382 25370018    4% /mnt/disk2
```

3. Finding the largest files and directories

To find the largest files and directories on your file system, you can use the du
command. The -h flag displays the sizes in human-readable format, and the -d flag
specifies the depth of the search.

For example, to find the largest files and directories in the current directory and its
subdirectories, you can use

```
$ du -h -d 1
4.0K    ./subdir1
24K     ./subdir2
8.0K    ./subdir3
48K     .
```

To find the largest files and directories on the entire file system, you can use:

```
$ sudo du -h -d 1 /
4.0K    /subdir1
24K     /subdir2
8.0K    /subdir3
12G     /
```

Working with Processes

A process is a running application instance in Linux and other operating systems. Every process executes in a different memory space and has its own distinct process ID (PID).

There are a few types of processes in Linux Operating Systems.

1. foreground processes: These are processes that are started from the command line and run in the foreground, meaning they are attached to the terminal and take input from and output to the terminal.

2. Background processes: These are processes that are started from the command line with an & at the end of the command, or with the bg command. They run in the background, meaning they are not attached to the terminal and do not take input from or output to the terminal.

3. Daemon processes: These are processes that run in the background and are not associated with a terminal. They are usually started at boot time and continue running until the system is shut down. Examples of daemon processes include the sshd daemon for handling SSH connections and the httpd daemon for serving web pages.

4. Orphan processes: These are processes that are started by a parent process but are no longer being controlled by that parent process. Orphan processes are adopted by the init process, which is the parent of all processes on the system.

5. Zombie processes: These are processes that have completed execution but are still listed in the process table because their parent process has not yet read their exit status. Zombie processes can be recognized by the Z state in the ps command output. They do not consume any system resources and can be safely ignored

6. Kernel threads: These are special processes that are created and managed by the kernel to perform specific tasks. They do not have a user-space memory address space and are not visible in the process table.

Commands to manipulate Linux Processes.

1. Viewing processes

   You may use the **ps** command to see the processes that are active on your system. For instance, you may use the ps aux command to examine every process that is currently active on your system. The PID, the user who owns the process, and the command that was used to start the process will all be shown in this way.

2. Killing processes

   You might occasionally need to end a process if it isn't responding or has ceased functioning. Use the **kill** command and the PID of the process you wish to end in order to do this. For instance, the command **kill 1234** will notify the process with PID 1234 to terminate.

   If the kill command doesn't work, try using the **kill -9** command, which forces the process to terminate by sending it a SIGKILL signal. However, if the process was in the middle of writing to a file, exercise caution when executing this command since it may result in data loss or corruption.

3. Starting and stopping processes

   You may just run the command for the application you wish to launch to begin a process. Run the **firefox** command, for instance, to launch the Firefox web browser.

   You can use the stop or kill command followed by the PID of the background-running process to end it.

4. Managing services

   Some applications are configured to operate on Linux systems as services, which are background processes that are launched at boot time. You may use the **systemctl** command to manage services on your computer.

For example, to start the Nginx web server service, you can use the command **systemctl start Nginx**. To stop the service, you can use the command **systemctl stop nginx**. To view the status of a service, you can use the command **systemctl status nginx**. Likewise, you can check the status or start/stop/restart almost any service using systemsctl.

Configuring SSH Connection

SSH (Secure Shell) is a network protocol used to securely connect to a remote computer. It is used to safely connect to a distant computer. It is frequently used to connect remotely to servers running Linux or Unix. Here is a simple tutorial for setting up SSH on a Linux computer:

Make sure your Linux computer has the OpenSSH-server package installed first. If it isn't already installed, you can do so by using your distribution package manager (e.g. apt-get on Ubuntu or yum on CentOS).

```
sudo apt-get update
sudo apt-get install openssh-server
```

The next step is to create a public and private key pair for your computer. Running the ssh-keygen program and following the on-screen instructions will do this. The password you enter must be kept in mind since you will need it to connect to the server.

```
ssh-keygen -t rsa
```

You must copy the public key to the remote system you wish to connect to after the key pair has been generated. s sh-copy-id could be used to do this. ssh-copy-id user@remote host, for instance.

```
ssh-copy-id user@remote_host
```

You should now be able to use SSH to connect to the remote system. Use the ssh command to accomplish this, then enter the username and remote hostname or IP address. ssh user@remote host, for instance. You will be asked to enter the key pair's passphrase.

```
ssh user@remote_host
```

You can make a different key pair and go through the process again for every user if you wish to enable SSH access for more than one user.

Configuring VNC Connection

Virtual Network Computing (VNC) is a technology that enables network-based remote computer control. When you need to use a computer remotely, such as when working from home or while traveling, it can be helpful.

With VNC, you may connect to a distant computer and virtually sit in front of it to view its desktop. The remote computer can then be managed using your keyboard and mouse, just as if you were in front of it. This enables you to use and access your files, programs, and other resources as though you were sitting at your workstation.

You may require VNC for a variety of reasons. You may need to, for instance:

- Remotely access a work computer from home
- Provide technical support to someone remotely
- Administer a server or other networked device
- Access your home computer from a different location

VNC is a helpful tool for anyone who needs to access and control a computer remotely in general. You can stay connected and productive from anywhere with it because it is simple to set up and use.

Here are the steps to follow to get a VNC server installed on a ubuntu server.

1. Install VNC Server:

   There are many options to use such as TigerVNC, UltraVNC, RealVN and etc. In this example we will demonstrate the TigerVNC installation on a Ubuntu-based system.

   ```
   sudo apt-get install tightvncserver
   ```

2. Configure VNC Server:

   This usually involves choosing the resolution of the remote desktop and creating a password for the VNC connection. For instance, you may use the following command to set a password for TightVNC on a machine running Ubuntu.

   ```
   tightvncserver :1 -passwd yourpassword
   ```

3. On the machine you'll be using to access the remote desktop, install a VNC client. For instance, you can use the following command to install TightVNC on a machine running Ubuntu:

   ```
   sudo apt-get install xtightvncviewer
   ```

   A VNC Client may also be installed on a Windows PC. You may utilize TightVNC, for instance. It is a Windows-compatible, open-source VNC client that is free.

Working with tar.gz compressed files

In Linux, tar stands for Tape Archive. It is a command line utility used to create and manipulate archive files. An archive is a single file that contains multiple files and directories. The tar utility is commonly used to create .tar archive files, but it can also be used to create .tar.gz (also called "tarballs") and other types of archives.

The tar command has many options and flags that allow you to specify how the archive should be created and what should be included in it. For example, you can use the -c flag to create a new archive, the -x flag to extract files from an existing archive, and the -v flag to display the names of the files as they are processed.

In addition to creating and extracting archives, the tar command can also be used to list the contents of an archive, add new files to an existing archive, and more. It is a very powerful tool that is widely used in the Linux world.

1. Navigate to the directory where the .tar.gz file is located. You can use the **cd** command to change directories. For example, if the file is located in the "Downloads" directory, you can use the command **cd Downloads** to navigate there.

2. Use the tar command to extract the .tar.gz file. The basic syntax is

```
tar -xvzf file.tar.gz
```

Here is what each flag does:

    x: This flag tells tar to extract the files.
    v: The v stands for "verbose." This flag tells tar to display the names of the files as it extracts them.
    z: This flag tells tar to uncompress the archive using gzip.
    f: This flag tells tar to use the following argument as the file name.

So, for example, if the name of your file is "example.tar.gz", you would use the following command:

```
tar -xvzf example.tar.gz
```

This will extract the contents of the .tar.gz file into the current directory.

3. If you want to extract the files to a specific directory, you can use the -C flag followed by the directory path. For example:

```
tar -xvzf example.tar.gz -C /path/to/extract/to
```

This will extract the contents of the .tar.gz file to the specified directory.

Must know Linux Shortcuts

There are a bundle of shortcuts available for Linux distributions. We will discuss about a few down below. Main two types of the shortcuts I'm discussing today is shortcuts on GUI(Graphical User Interface) and shortcuts on CLI(Command Line Interface).

Common shortcuts for GUI

When using a computer, using shortcuts may increase your productivity and efficiency. You may utilize shortcuts to do activities more quickly and effectively by avoiding the need to use a mouse or travel through menus. You may be able to work more swiftly and effectively as a result of this. Additionally, since you won't have to alternate between the keyboard and mouse all the time, employing shortcuts might assist lessen the stress on your hands and wrists. In general, learning shortcuts may increase your computer productivity and efficiency.

Below are a few of common shortcuts available in Linux

1. Ctrl + Alt + T: This shortcut will open a new terminal window.
2. Ctrl + Shift + T: This shortcut will open a new tab in the terminal window.
3. Ctrl + L: This shortcut will clear the terminal window.
4. Ctrl + D: This shortcut will close the terminal window.
5. Ctrl + Z: This shortcut will suspend the current process.
6. Ctrl + C: This shortcut will kill the current process.
7. Ctrl + Shift + C: This shortcut will copy the selected text.
8. Ctrl + Shift + V: This shortcut will paste the copied text.
9. Tab: This shortcut will auto-complete a command or file name.
10. Up arrow: This shortcut will recall the previous command.

11. Down arrow: This shortcut will recall the next command.

Securely Copy Files Using SCP

Secure copy is abbreviated as "scp." Linux has a command-line tool that makes it possible to safely transfer data across a network between two machines. The data being exchanged is encrypted using the ssh protocol, keeping it safe and impervious to eavesdropping.

1. Open a terminal window on your local computer (the one you want to copy files FROM).

2. Make sure you have an ssh client installed on your local computer. Most Linux distributions come with an ssh client installed by default, but if you don't have one, you can install one using your package manager (e.g. **apt-get**, **yum**, etc.).

3. If you don't know the IP address or hostname of the remote server (the one you want to copy files TO), you can find it out by running the following command on the remote server:

```
hostname -I
```

4. To copy a file from your local computer to the remote server, use the following scp command:

```
scp /path/to/local/file username@remote_server:/path/to/remote/destination
```

5. Replace **/path/to/local/file** with the path to the file on your local computer, **username** with your username on the remote server, **remote_server** with the IP address or hostname of the remote server, and **/path/to/remote/destination** with the path to the destination on the remote server where you want to copy the file.

6. You will be prompted to enter your password for the remote server. Enter it and press Enter. The file will be securely copied to the remote server.

7. To copy a file from the remote server to your local computer, use the following **scp** command:

```
scp username@remote_server:/path/to/remote/file /path/to/local/destination
```

Here are a few different commands you may use in Linux to transfer data across computers:

1. **rsync:** This is a robust program that enables file synchronization between two computers. It offers a wide range of choices for fine-tuning the synchronization procedure, including the capacity to choose a different remote shell to use, exclude particular files or directories, and more.
2. **sftp:** The term "secure file transfer protocol" is abbreviated as "sftp." It is a command-line tool that enables file transfers through an ssh connection between machines. Although it uses a syntax similar to ftp, it encrypts the data being sent to increase its security.
3. **sshfs:** You can mount a remote filesystem using sshfs, a filesystem client, through an ssh connection. Once the remote filesystem is mounted, you may use common Linux commands like cp, mv, rm, etc. to view the files on it just like any other local filesystem.

Package Managers for Linux

A contemporary Linux distribution is made up of a variety of packages (libraries, applications, documentation, etc.), all of which may be installed, updated, and managed with the use of software tools called package managers. APT (Advanced Packaging Tool), used by Debian and Ubuntu, YUM (Yellowdog Updater, Modified), used by Red Hat and CentOS, and pacman, used by Arch Linux, are some of the most well-known package managers for Linux. Installing new packages and their dependencies is made simple by package managers, which also let you keep track of installed packages and their versions and update them when newer versions are released. The trouble of manually obtaining, creating, and installing packages from source code is also reduced thanks to them.

1. Install a package: **yum install <package_name>**
2. Update a package: **yum update <package_name>**
3. Upgrade all installed packages to their latest versions: **yum upgrade**
4. Remove a package: **yum remove <package_name>**
5. Search for a package: **yum search <package_name>**
6. List installed packages: **yum list installed**

Sample commands using 'apt'

1. Install a package: **apt-get install <package_name>**
2. Update package database and installed packages: **apt-get update && apt-get upgrade**
3. Remove a package: **apt-get remove <package_name>**
4. Search for a package: **apt-cache search <package_name>**
5. List installed packages: **apt list --installed**

GUI Tools for Linux System Administrators.

Cockpit: For Linux servers, Cockpit is a web-based system administration application. For carrying out typical system administration duties, such controlling services, checking system logs, and keeping track of resource utilization, it offers a user-friendly interface. Cockpit has a number of features, including System dashboard, Service management, System logs, Storage management, Network configuration and etc.

Gnome System Monitor: An summary of the system's resource utilization, including CPU, memory, and network usage, is provided by this program. You may also observe and control processes, keep an eye on system functions, and more.

KDE System Guard: Although it is a component of the KDE desktop environment, this utility is comparable to Gnome System Monitor. You may examine and control processes and system services as well as get an overview of how the system is using its resources.

GParted: Disk partitions are managed with this utility. It supports filesystems like ext2, ext3, and ext4 and allows you to create, remove, and resize partitions.

YaST (Yet another Setup Tool): This program is a system configuration tool that you may use to set up your system's networking, software administration, and system services, among other features. Only systems running the SUSE Linux operating system may access it.

Synaptic Package Manager: The APT package management system's graphical front-end is represented by this utility. It offers features for maintaining and upgrading installed packages in addition to letting you search for and install software packages.

Best Command Line HTTP Clients for Linux

Command-line HTTP clients are tools that allow you to make HTTP requests from the command line, rather than using a graphical user interface (GUI). These tools are often used by developers and system administrators to automate tasks or to quickly test HTTP-based APIs. They are also useful for debugging web applications, as they allow you to see the raw HTTP request and response data

Using a command-line HTTP client, you can make HTTP requests to a web server, retrieve data from a website, or send data to a server. You can also use command-line HTTP clients to test the performance of a web server or to measure the response time of a web application.

There are many different command-line HTTP clients available for Linux, each with its own unique features and capabilities. Some popular examples include cURL, HTTPie, Wget, and Httpie

1. **cURL**: One of the most widely-used command-line HTTP clients, cURL is a free, open-source tool that can be used to make HTTP requests from the command line. It supports a wide range of protocols, including HTTP, HTTPS, FTP, and more.

2. **Wget**: A popular command-line HTTP client that is widely used for downloading files from the web. It is known for its ability to download files over HTTP, HTTPS, and FTP, and can also be used to make HTTP requests from the command line.

3. **Httpie**: Another user-friendly command-line HTTP client that is similar to cURL in terms of its capabilities. It is easy to use and has a syntax that is more intuitive for many users.

Best IP Address Management Tools for Linux

Tools for managing IP addresses are used to schedule, assign, and track their use on a network. They are crucial for network managers because they enable them to effectively control the distribution of IP addresses to networked devices and resolve any connection problems.

The following are some typical tasks that IP address management software can be used for:

- Assigning static or dynamic IP addresses to devices
- Monitoring the use of IP addresses on a network to ensure that there are enough available for new devices
- Tracking which devices are using which IP addresses
- Configuring the routing table to direct traffic to the correct destinations
- Monitoring and blocking suspicious network activity
- Troubleshooting connectivity issues

By using IP address management tools, network administrators can ensure that their networks are running smoothly and efficiently, and can quickly resolve any issues that may arise.

Below are a few of the IP address management tools available.
iproute2: This is a suite of utilities for managing network interfaces, IP addresses, and the routing table. It is included in most Linux distributions by default.

ifconfig: This is a command-line tool for displaying and configuring network interface parameters. It is also included in most Linux distributions by default.

dhcpd: This is the DHCP server daemon for Linux systems. It can be used to automatically assign IP addresses to clients on a network.

dnsmasq: This is a lightweight DNS and DHCP server. It is commonly used on home networks and small businesses.

iptables: This is a firewall utility for Linux systems that can be used to control incoming and outgoing network traffic.

nmap: This is a security tool that can be used to scan networks and perform IP address management tasks, such as finding open ports and detecting operating systems.

arpwatch: This is a tool that monitors Address Resolution Protocol (ARP) activity on a network and sends notifications when changes are detected.

fping: This is a command-line utility that can be used to ping multiple hosts at once and display the results in real-time.

ipcalc: This is a command-line tool that can be used to perform IP address calculations, such as calculating subnet masks and broadcast addresses.

Open Source Log Monitoring and Management Tools

In order to discover problems and trends, as well as to make decision-making and problem-solving easier, log monitoring systems are used to gather, process, and analyze log data.

A log monitoring system may be used for a variety of reasons, including

- Detecting and alerting on errors and issues: Log monitoring systems can be configured to send alerts when specific errors or issues are detected in log data, allowing you to quickly address problems before they become serious.
- Debugging and troubleshooting: Log data can be used to help identify the root cause of issues and to find solutions to problems.
- Performance monitoring: Log data can be used to monitor the performance of systems and applications, and to identify potential bottlenecks or other issues.
- Compliance: In some cases, log data may need to be collected and retained for compliance purposes, and a log monitoring system can make it easier to manage this data.
- Security: Log data can be used to monitor for security breaches and suspicious activity, and to help identify and respond to

Overall, log monitoring systems can help ensure that systems and applications are functioning properly, identify and address problems in a timely manner, and provide valuable insights for making informed decisions

There are many open source log monitoring and management tools available for Linux. Here are a few popular ones:

- Logwatch: This is a log analysis tool that parses log files and generates reports based on them. It can be configured to send reports via email or to a file.
- Nagios Log Server: This is a log management tool that allows you to search, filter, and analyze log data in real-time. It also offers alerting capabilities and can be integrated with other Nagios tools.

- Graylog: This is a log management platform that allows you to collect, index, and analyze log data from a variety of sources. It offers a web interface for searching and analyzing logs, as well as alerting capabilities.
- Splunk: This is a log analysis tool that allows you to search, analyze, and visualize log data. It offers a range of features, including real-time searching, alerting, and dashboards.

- Kibana: This is a visualization tool for analyzing and exploring log data. It is often used in conjunction with Elasticsearch, a search and analytics engine.

Backup Utilities for Linux Systems

Data security, disaster recovery, and protection against data loss are all made possible through backups. They let you to recover from unanticipated events like hardware breakdowns, software defects, malicious attacks, and other situations that may otherwise lead to the loss of critical information. They also assist in ensuring compliance with regulations that can mandate that companies maintain copies of their data. You can protect your data and maintain the efficiency of your organization by putting in place a solid backup system.

Below are a few simple ways of creating backups in a Linux Operating System.

- **tar**: This is a utility that creates a single file called a tarball, which contains all the files and directories you want to backup. You can use the -czvf options to create a compressed tarball.
- **rsync**: This is a utility that syncs files and directories between two locations. It is often used to create backups, because it only copies over files that have changed, which makes it efficient.
- **cp**: This is a basic Linux utility that can be used to copy files and directories. It's not as powerful as tar or rsync, but it can be useful for simple backup tasks.
- **dump**: This is a utility that can be used to create backups of a file system. It can handle things like hard links and special file types, which can be useful when backing up certain types of systems.
- **dd**: This is a utility that can be used to create a raw image of a disk or partition. It can be useful for creating backups of entire systems, but it is not as flexible as some of the other utilities mentioned above.
- **rsnapshot**: This is a utility that uses rsync to create incremental backups of a file system. It can be configured to keep a specified number of versions of each file, which makes it easy to restore a file to a previous version if needed.

Backup Programs for Linux

The creation of backups of files, directories, and systems is done using backup utilities, which are command-line programs. They may be set up using configuration files and command-line parameters, and are often launched from the command line. The backup tools tar, rsync, cp, and dd are a few examples.

On the other hand, backup solutions typically come in the form of graphical programs that offer a user-friendly interface for generating and maintaining backups. They frequently have more features and capabilities than backup tools, and they may support many storage backends and include features like scheduling, compression, and encryption. Backup software includes, for instance, Duplicity, Bacula, Areca, and Back In Time.

Backup utilities are best suited for activities that demand a high level of customization or automation since they are often more straightforward and lightweight than backup programs. On the other hand, backup programs are more feature-rich, user-friendly, and better suited for jobs that call for a more user-friendly interface.

Duplicity: This tool makes incremental backups of files and directories using the rsync algorithm. It may be set up to store backups on many different storage backends, such as local drives, remote servers, and cloud storage services.

Bacula: This tool for creating backups of files, folders, and complete systems is available for free. You may personalize your backups thanks to the setup system's intricate yet adaptable features..

Areca: This graphical backup tool has an easy-to-use interface that enables you to make backups of your files and folders. Numerous storage backends, including local drives, remote servers, and cloud storage providers, are supported.

Back In Time: You may use this straightforward backup tool to make incremental backups of your files and folders. It may be set to store backups on local drives or remote servers and features a graphical user interface..

```
Server:     127.0.1.1
Address:    127.0.1.1#53

Non-authoritative answer:
Name:   example.com
Address: 93.184.216.34
```

Manage Networking with Network Manager in RHEL/CentOS

Network Manager is a service that controls the network settings on your system in Red Hat
Enterprise Linux (RHEL) and CentOS. It may be used to control and manage network
connections as well as to set up and configure network interfaces. It is intended for Network
Manager to take the role of the traditional **ifup** and **ifdown** programs that are used to setup
network interfaces in these operating systems. Network Manager may be used to manage both
wired and wireless network connections.

- You must install the **NetworkManager** package, which is accessible from the default
  repositories, in order to utilize Network Manager on RHEL/CentOS. Run the following
  command to launch the Network Manager service after the package has been installed.

```
systemctl start NetworkManager
```

- You can then use the nmcli command-line tool to manage network settings and
  connections. For example, to list the available network connections, you can use the
  nmcli connection command.

```
nmcli connection
```

- The **nmcli connection add** command can be used to establish a new network connection. For example, you may use the following command to make a new wired Ethernet connection.

```
nmcli connection add type ethernet con-name "My Ethernet Connection" ifname eth0
```

- You can also use the nmcli tool to control and manage network connections. For example, to activate a connection, you can use the nmcli connection up command.

```
nmcli connection up "My Ethernet Connection"
```

- To deactivate a connection, you can use the nmcli connection down command.

```
nmcli connection down "My Ethernet Connection"
```

Set Static IP Address on CentOS/RHEL

To set a static IP address on a CentOS or RHEL system, you will need to edit the network configuration files for the network interface that you want to configure.

The network configuration files for each network interface are stored in the **/etc/sysconfig/network-scripts** directory, and are named **ifcfg-<interface>**, where <interface> is the name of the network interface (e.g. **ifcfg-eth0** for the first Ethernet interface).

To set a static IP address on a network interface, you will need to edit the configuration file for that interface and set the **BOOTPROTO** parameter to **none**, and set the **IPADDR** parameter to the static IP address that you want to use. For example:

```
BOOTPROTO=none
IPADDR=192.168.1.100
```

You will also need to set the NETMASK parameter to the appropriate netmask for your network, and the GATEWAY parameter to the IP address of your default gateway. For example:

```
NETMASK=255.255.255.0
GATEWAY=192.168.1.1
```

Once you have edited the configuration file, you will need to restart the network service to apply the changes. You can do this by running the following command:

```
systemctl restart network
```

Alternatively, you can use the **nmcli** command-line tool to set a static IP address on a network interface. For example, to set a static IP address on the **eth0** interface, you can use the following command:

```
nmcli connection modify eth0 ipv4.method manual ipv4.addresses
"192.168.1.100/24" ipv4.gateway "192.168.1.1"
```

This will set the static IP address of **192.168.1.100** with a netmask of **255.255.255.0** (/24) and a default gateway of **192.168.1.1** on the **eth0** interface. You will need to restart the network service for the changes to take effect.

Below is a full sample interface configuration file.

```
DEVICE=eth0
BOOTPROTO=none
ONBOOT=yes
IPADDR=192.168.1.100
NETMASK=255.255.255.0
GATEWAY=192.168.1.1
DNS1=8.8.8.8
DNS2=8.8.4.4
```

For more information on configuring network settings in CentOS and RHEL, you can refer to the documentation: https://access.redhat.com/documentation/en-US/Red_Hat_Enterprise_Linux/7/html/Networking_Guide/index.html

File and Disk Encryption Tools for Linux

Encrypting files and disks is crucial because it shields your data from illegal access. In the event that your computer or portable storage device is lost, stolen, or if someone tries to access your sensitive data without your permission, it is crucial to safeguard that information.

Your files and drives can be protected by encryption so that even if someone manages to access your device, they won't be able to view the data without the right decryption key. This can aid in the prevention of online crimes such as financial fraud and identity theft.

Additionally, encrypted data might be helpful in circumstances when you must adhere to rules or guidelines that demand the security of sensitive information, such as the GDPR in the European Union or HIPAA in the healthcare sector.

Encrypting files and disks can add an extra degree of protection to help safeguard your data and prevent illegal access.

There are a number of file and disk encryption tools available for Linux, including:

GnuPG (GNU Privacy Guard): a free software implementation of the OpenPGP standard for encrypting and signing data.

dmcrypt: a kernel-level encryption module for the Linux kernel that can be used to create encrypted volumes.

TrueCrypt: a cross-platform, open-source encryption program that can create encrypted volumes or encrypt an entire hard drive. It is no longer actively maintained.

LUKS (Linux Unified Key Setup): the standard for Linux hard disk encryption. It allows users to secure their data by creating a virtual encrypted volume within a file or on a partition.

eCryptfs: a free, open-source disk encryption system for Linux that is included in the Linux kernel. It allows users to create encrypted directories that can be mounted and accessed like any other directory.

Cryptsetup: a free, open-source disk encryption utility that is used to set up dm-crypt and LUKS-based encrypted volumes.

VeraCrypt: a fork of the discontinued TrueCrypt project that adds additional security features and is actively maintained.

Cron Jobs for Linux

Cron is a Linux utility that allows users to schedule tasks to be executed automatically at a specified time or interval. These tasks are called "cron jobs." Cron reads the configuration files located in the /etc/cron.* directories to determine which commands to execute and when to execute them.

To create a cron job, you need to specify two things: the schedule and the command to be executed. The schedule is defined using a series of special symbols that indicate when the job should be run. For example, to run a job every day at midnight, you would use the following schedule: 0 0 * * *. The command to be executed can be any valid shell command.

To create a cron job, you can use the crontab command. For example, to create a cron job that runs the backup.sh script every day at midnight, you would use the following command:

```
crontab -e
```

This will open the crontab file in your default text editor. Add the following line to the file

```
0 0 * * * /path/to/backup.sh
```

Using the resources below, you may learn more about creating cron tasks at every level, from beginner to experienced administrator. The websites listed below provide sophisticated tools that can assist you in creating cronjobs.

- https://www.freeformatter.com/
- https://crontab.guru/

Run a Command with Time Limit (Timeout) In Linux

To run a command with a time limit in Linux, you can use the timeout command.

For example, to run the sleep command for a maximum of 5 seconds, you can use the following command:

```
timeout 5 sleep 10
```

If the **sleep 10** command is performed by the **timeout** command and the command doesn't end after 5 seconds, the process is killed and the command exits.

With the '**--signal**' argument of the **timeout** command, a different signal can be specified to be sent to the process when the time limit is reached. For instance, you may use the following command to notify the process that the time limit has been reached by sending it the SIGINT signal (which is equivalent to pressing CTRL+C):

```
timeout --signal=SIGINT 5 sleep 10
```

Note that the timeout command is not available on all Linux systems. On systems that don't have the timeout command, you can use the bash builtin time command to achieve a similar effect.

```
time bash -c "sleep 10"
```

This will run the command sleep 10 in a new instance of bash, and the time command will display the elapsed time when the command finishes or is terminated. You can use the kill command to send a signal to the sleep process if it hasn't finished within the desired time limit.

For example, to run the sleep command for a maximum of 5 seconds and send the SIGINT signal to the process if it hasn't finished by then, you can use the following script,

```bash
#!/bin/bash

# Start the sleep command in the background
sleep 10 &

# Save the process ID of the sleep command
sleep_pid=$!

# Set a time limit of 5 seconds
time_limit=5

# Loop until the time limit is reached or the sleep command finishes
while [[ $time_limit -gt 0 ]] && kill -0 $sleep_pid 2>/dev/null; do
  sleep 1
  ((time_limit--))
done

# If the sleep command is still running, send it the SIGINT signal
if kill -0 $sleep_pid 2>/dev/null; then
  kill -SIGINT $sleep_pid
fi
```

Install Apache Tomcat on Debian

To install Apache Tomcat on Debian, follow these steps,

1. Download the latest stable version of Apache Tomcat from the Apache Tomcat website (http://tomcat.apache.org/)

2. Extract the downloaded file to the location where you want to install Tomcat. For example, to install Tomcat in the /opt/tomcat directory, use the following command:

```
tar xvf apache-tomcat-9*.tar.gz -C /opt/tomcat --strip-
components=1
```

3. Add a system user and group for Tomcat. This is optional, but it is a good practice to run Tomcat as a non-root user for security reasons. Run the following commands to add the tomcat user and group

```
sudo groupadd tomcat
sudo useradd -s /bin/false -g tomcat -d /opt/tomcat tomcat
```

4. Change the ownership of the Tomcat installation directory to the tomcat user and group

```
sudo chown -R tomcat:tomcat /opt/tomcat
```

5. Create a systemd service file for Tomcat. This will allow you to manage Tomcat as a service using the systemctl command. Create a file called tomcat.service in the /etc/systemd/system directory and add the following content to it,

```
[Unit]
Description=Apache Tomcat Web Application Container
After=network.target

[Service]
Type=forking

User=tomcat
Group=tomcat

Environment="JAVA_HOME=/usr/lib/jvm/default-java"
Environment="JAVA_OPTS=-Djava.security.egd=file:///dev/urandom"

ExecStart=/opt/tomcat/bin/startup.sh
ExecStop=/opt/tomcat/bin/shutdown.sh

Restart=on-failure
RestartSec=30

[Install]
WantedBy=multi-user.target
```

6. Reload the systemd daemon to pick up the new service file

```
sudo systemctl daemon-reload
```

7. Start the Tomcat service and enable it to start automatically on boot

```
sudo systemctl start tomcat
sudo systemctl enable tomcat
```

Now, Tomcat should be running on your system. You can verify this by accessing the Tomcat home page at **http://localhost:8080**